the Fratellis
Here We Stand

My Friend John ... 5
A Heady Tale ... 10
Shameless ... 18
Look Out Sunshine! ... 25
Stragglers Moon ... 32
Mistress Mabel ... 38
Jesus Stole Baby ... 45
Babydoll ... 51
Tell Me A Lie ... 58
Acid Jazz Singer ... 63
Lupe Brown ... 69
Milk And Money ... 76

© 2008 by International Music Publications Ltd
First published by International Music Publications Ltd in 2008
International Music Publications Ltd is a Faber Music company
3 Queen Square, London WC1N 3AU

Arranged by Alex Davis
Edited by Lucy Holliday

Design: Traffic
Cover Photography: Chip Simons
Band Photography: Scarlett Page
Logo: Mark James

Printed in England by Caligraving Ltd
All rights reserved

The text paper used in this publication is a virgin fibre product
that is manufactured in the UK to ISO 14001 standards.
The wood fibre used is only sourced from managed forests using
sustainable forestry principles. This paper is 100% recyclable

ISBN10: 0-571-53220-9
EAN13: 978-0-571-53220-9

To buy Faber Music publications or to find out about the full
range of titles available, please contact your local music retailer
or Faber Music sales enquiries:

Faber Music Ltd
Burnt Mill, Elizabeth Way, Harlow, CM20 2HX England
Tel:+44(0)1279 82 89 82 Fax:+44(0)1279 82 89 83
sales@fabermusic.com fabermusic.com

This is album is dedicated to Calum Macleod.

MY FRIEND JOHN

Words and Music by John Lawler

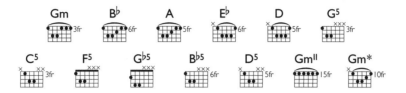

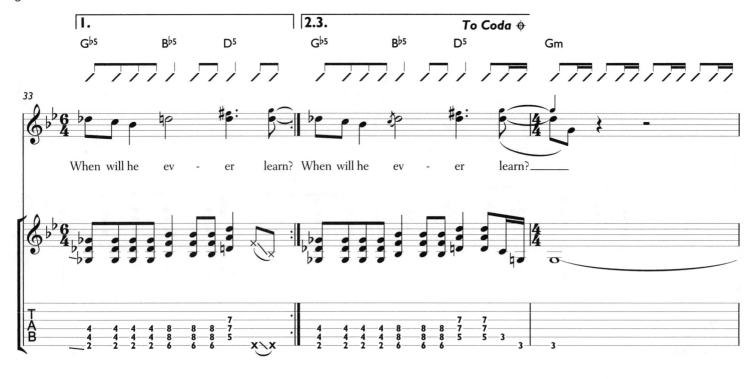

When will he ev - er learn? When will he ev - er learn?_____

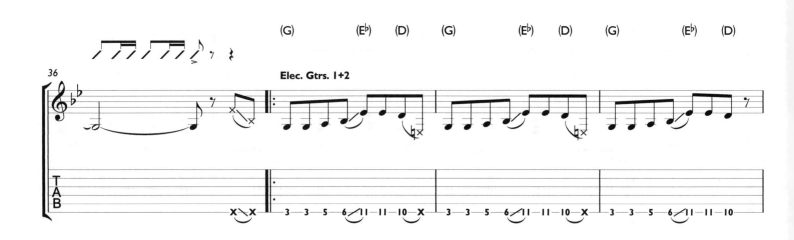

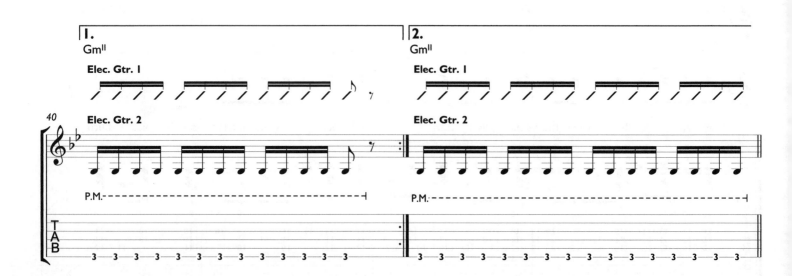

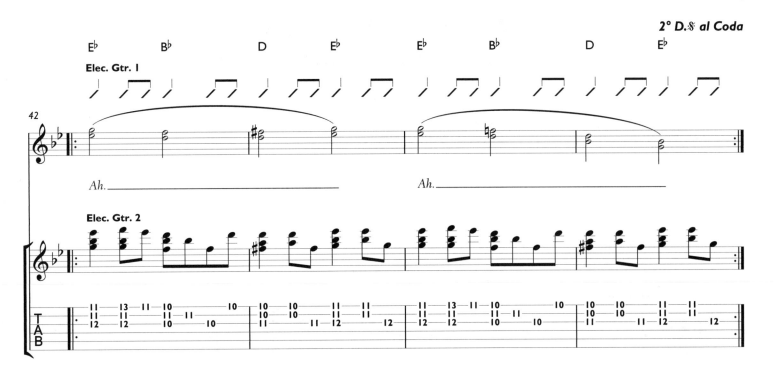

Ah._____ Ah._____

✛ Coda

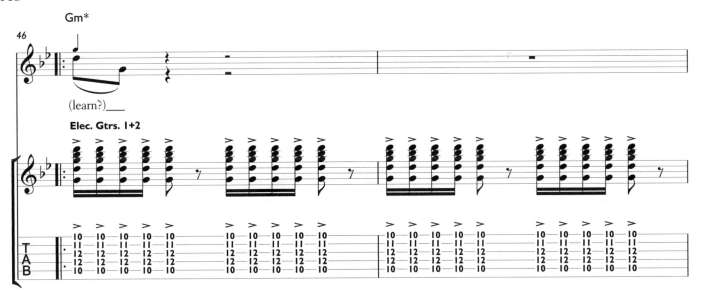

(learn?)____

A HEADY TALE

Words and Music by John Lawler

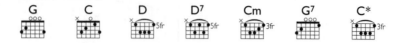

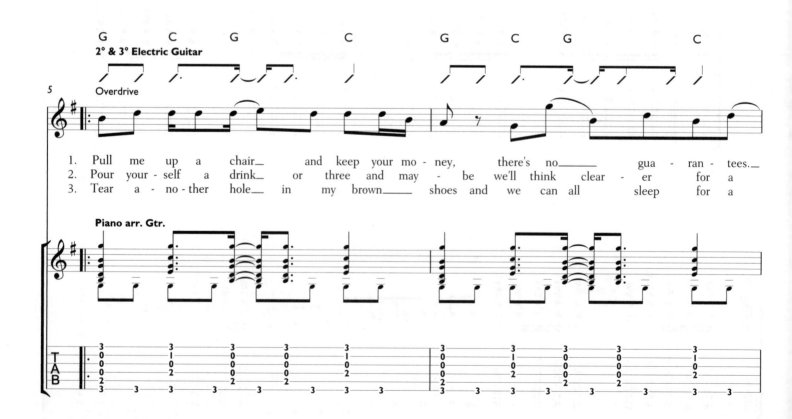

1. Pull me up a chair__ and keep your mo - ney, there's no_____ gua - ran - tees.
2. Pour your - self a drink__ or three and may - be we'll think clear - er for a
3. Tear a - no - ther hole__ in my brown_____ shoes and we can all sleep for a

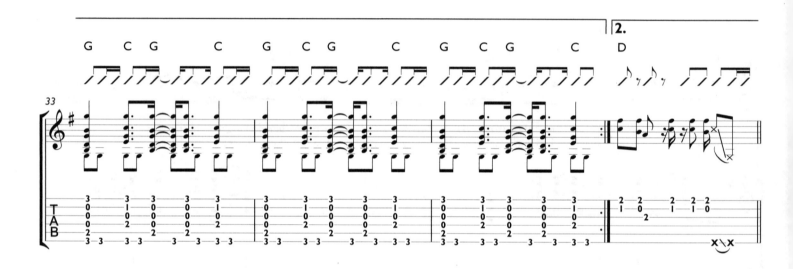

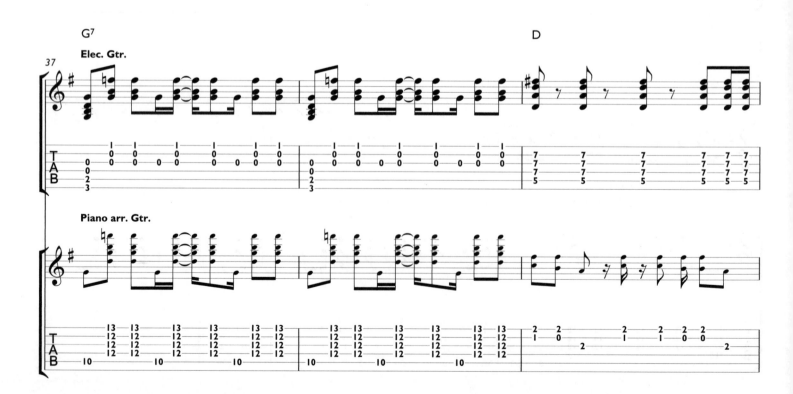

G C G C G C G C G
(3° only)
while.
while.
Well I
D D7 D D7 D D7 D D7
Won't you please for - give me, but you know cold blood - ed wo - men make me
You may be an em - bar - rass - ment, but I love the way your clothes are never in
told you once be - fore I love your bra - ces and your he - si - tant smile.
G C G C G C G C G C
sneeze.
style.
And I'll kick you out the door if for
Liv - ing's much too ea - sy, and
But please don't get me wrong, it's on - ly

So steal the

SHAMELESS

Words and Music by John Lawler

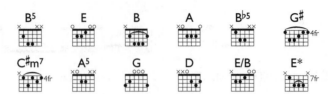

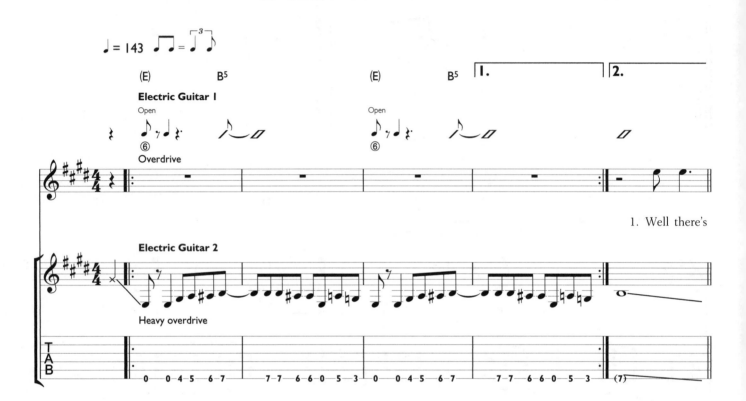

1. Well there's

no-thing more___ to add___ be - fore___ I leave.___ This

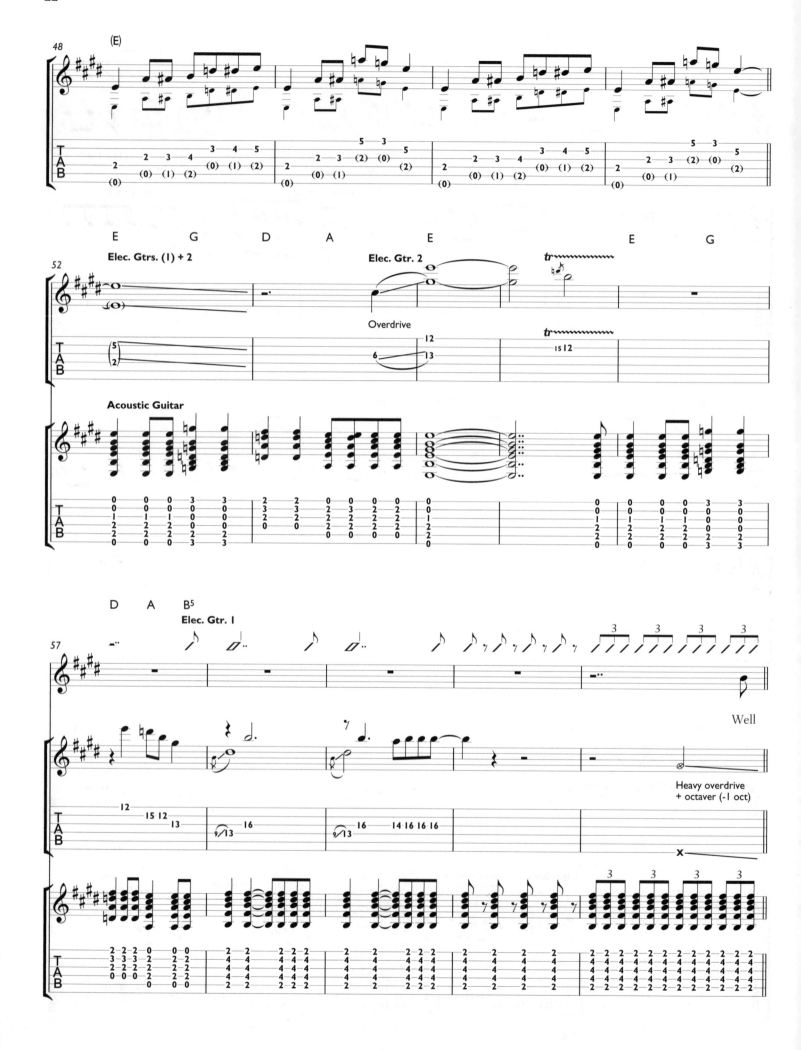

E
B5
(E)
B5
Elec. Gtr. 1
34
tell me you could do it if you tried.__ Well it's a
Elec. Gtrs. (1) + 2
Elec. Gtr. 2
E
G#
C#m7
B5
A5
Bb5
E
38
shame or a__ sham__ he's half as old__ as I__ am, but don't tell me he could
B5
(E)
E
43
(1° only)
look good if he tried.__ 2. Well it
Elec. Gtrs. 1 (small notes) + 2
TAB

tell me   he could look good if he   tried.___   2. And

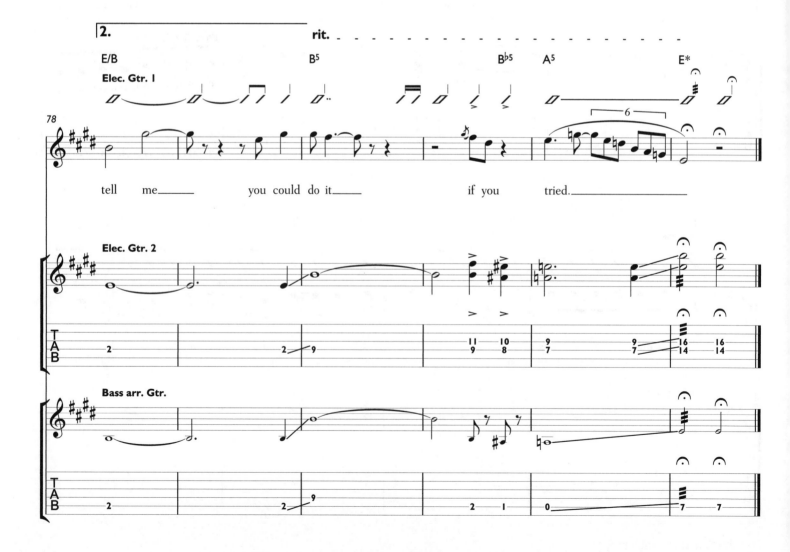

tell me___   you could do it___   if you   tried._____

LOOK OUT SUNSHINE!

Words and Music by John Lawler

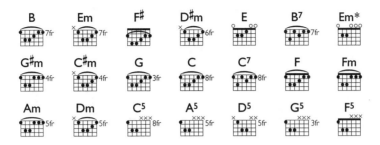

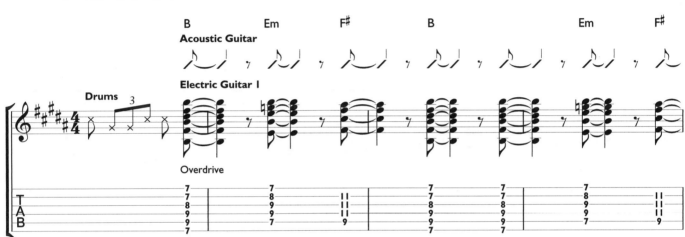

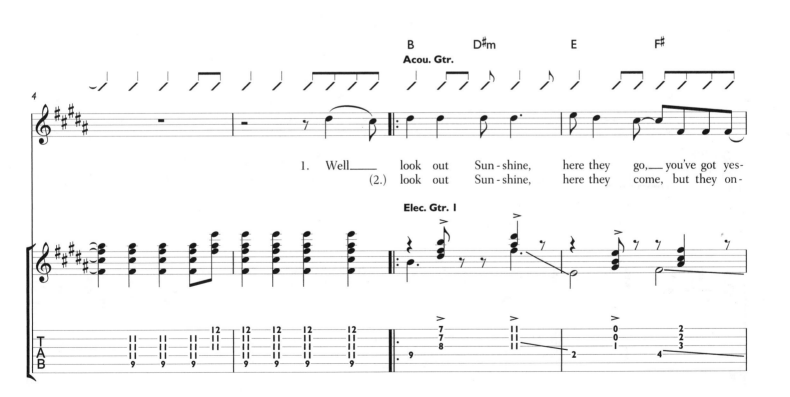

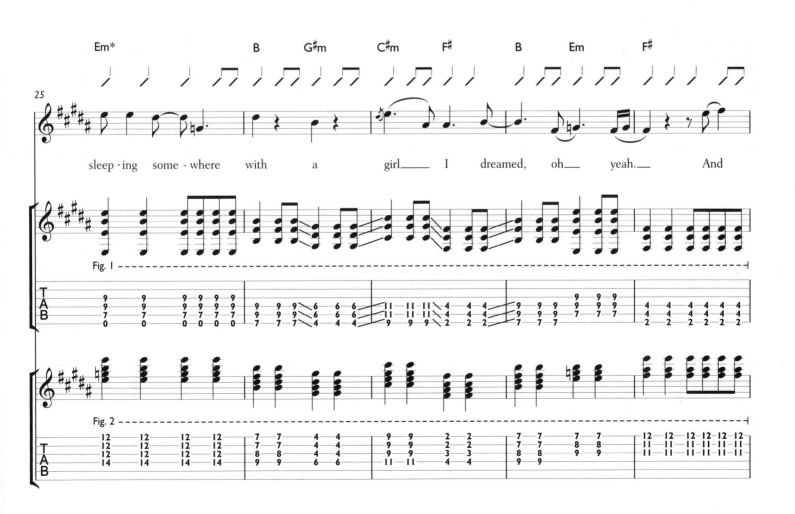

Tell___ my___ friends   I'll   be a -

- round._____   And

STRAGGLERS MOON

Words and Music by Bobby Troup and John Lawler

She can't help it, the girl can't help it. She can't help it, the girl can't help it.

Elec. Gtr. 1 plays Fig. 2
2° Elec. Gtr. plays Fig. 4

1. You can find her scratch-ing a-round in the dark,_____
2. The wrong way round's the right way up when she calls._____

just a-no-ther can-dle cha-sing a spark._____
You can laugh but it won't mean no-thing at all._____

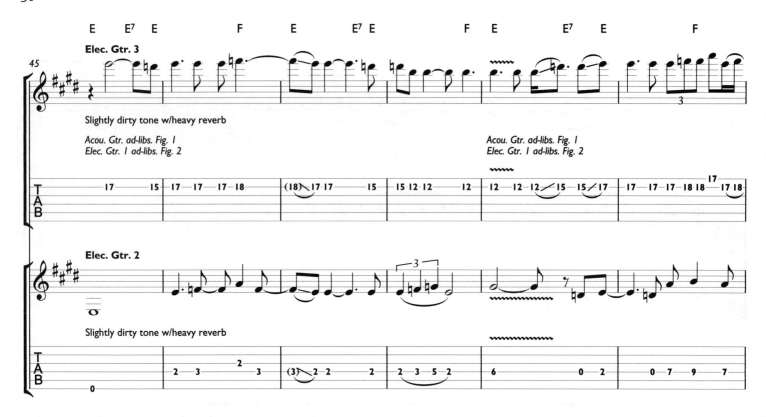

D.%. al Coda

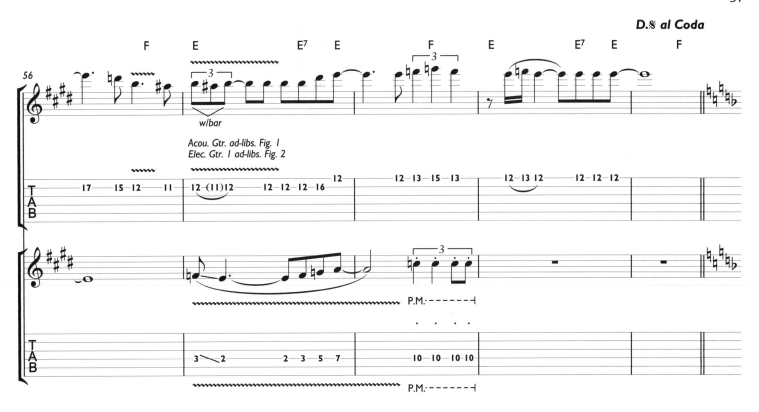

Coda

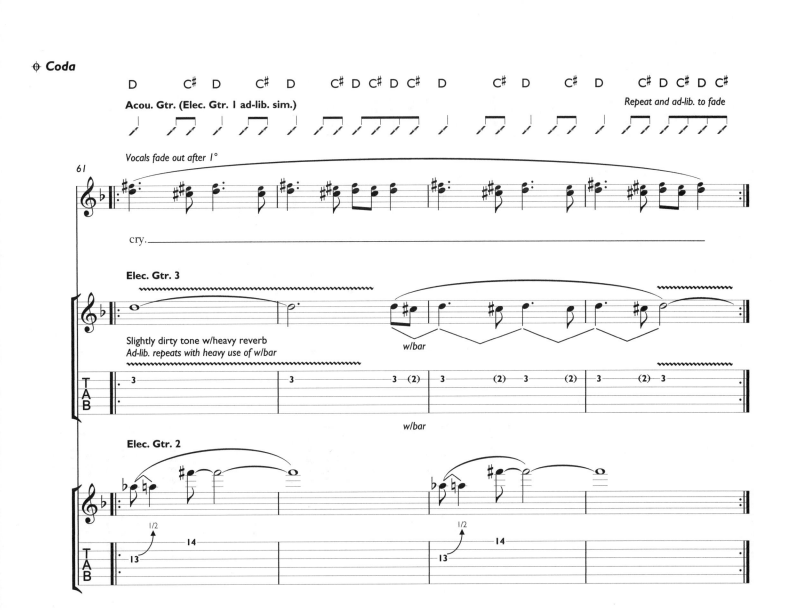

MISTRESS MABEL
Words and Music by John Lawler

One, two, three, aaow!

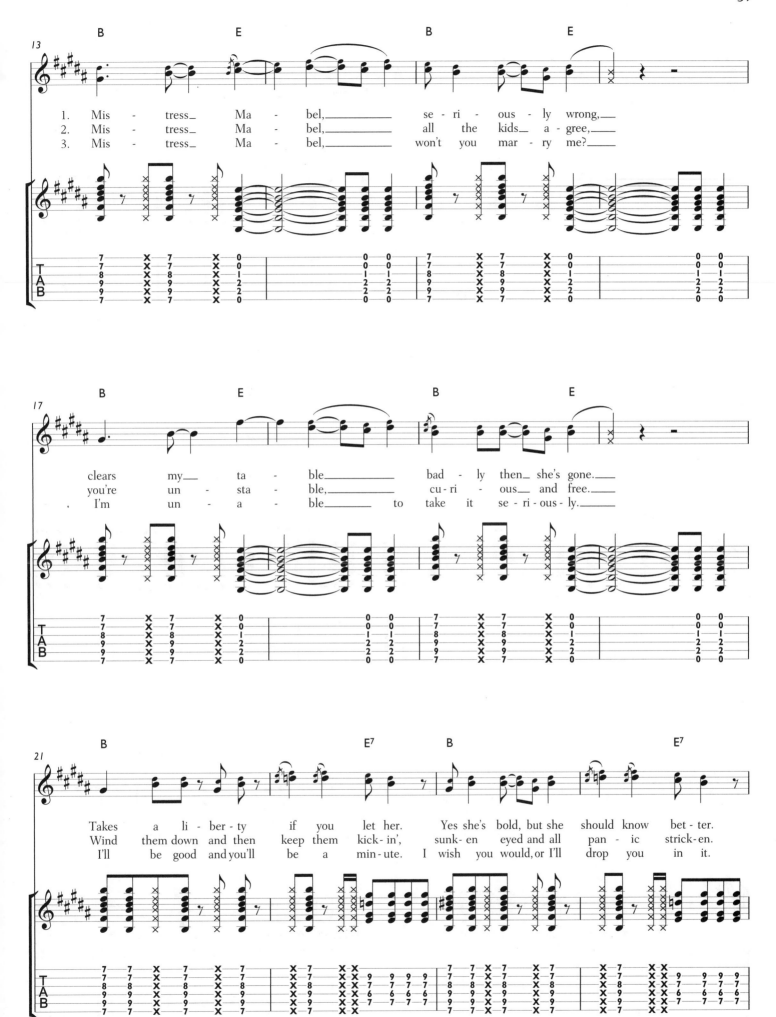

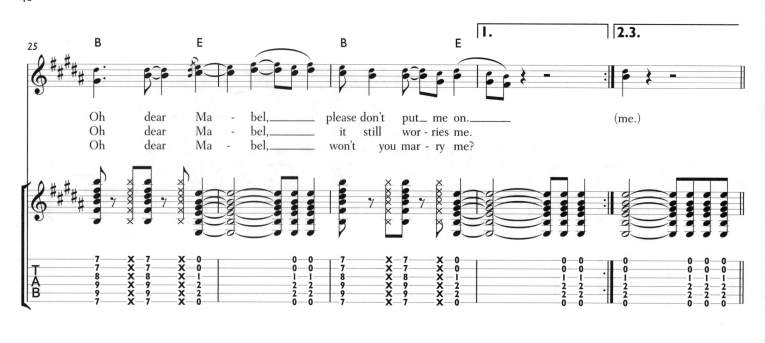

Oh dear Ma - bel,_____ please don't put_ me on._____ (me.)
Oh dear Ma - bel,_____ it still wor - ries me.
Oh dear Ma - bel,_____ won't you mar - ry me?

Hem line__ rat bag so__ they told__ her. Last nights name__ tag ac -

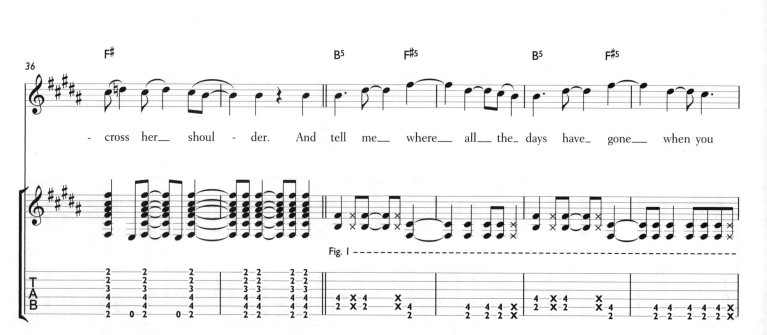

- cross her__ shoul - der. And tell me__ where__ all__ the_ days have_ gone__ when you

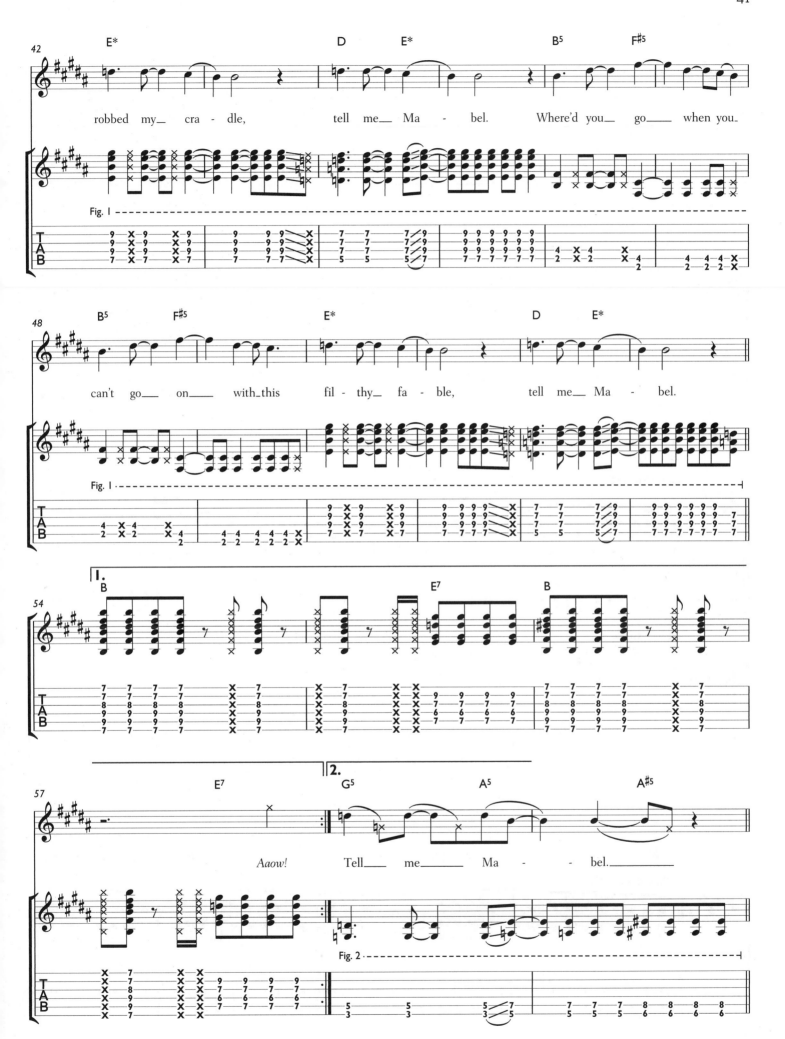

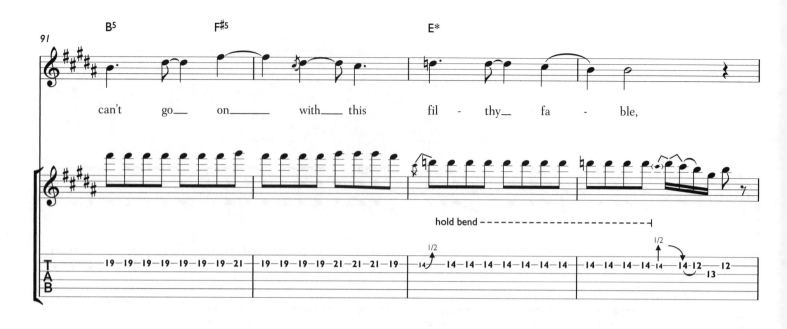

can't go on with this fil - thy fa - ble,

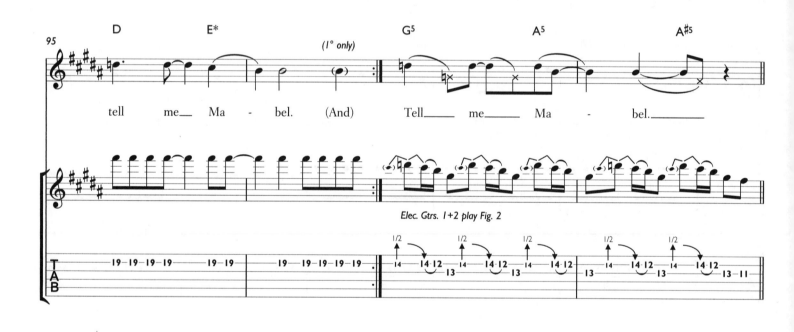

tell me Ma - bel. (And) Tell me Ma - bel.

Elec. Gtrs. 1+2 play Fig. 2

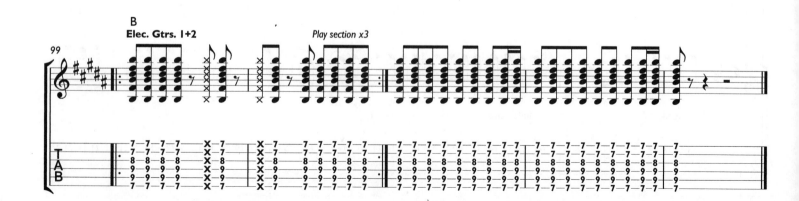

JESUS STOLE MY BABY

Words and Music by John Lawler

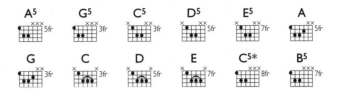

1. Je-sus stole my ba - by, ... Je-sus stole my girl,
2. She was al-ways ea - sy, ... se - ven days of the week,
3. Said that she just wants to save me, ... said you can't go the way that you are.
(4.) al-ways been in love with her trea - sure, ... but she might as well be locked up in chains.
(5.) I could on - ly talk to this Je - sus, ... I'd tell him just how lone - ly I've been.
6. Je-sus stole my ba - by, ... so may-be I should steal his.

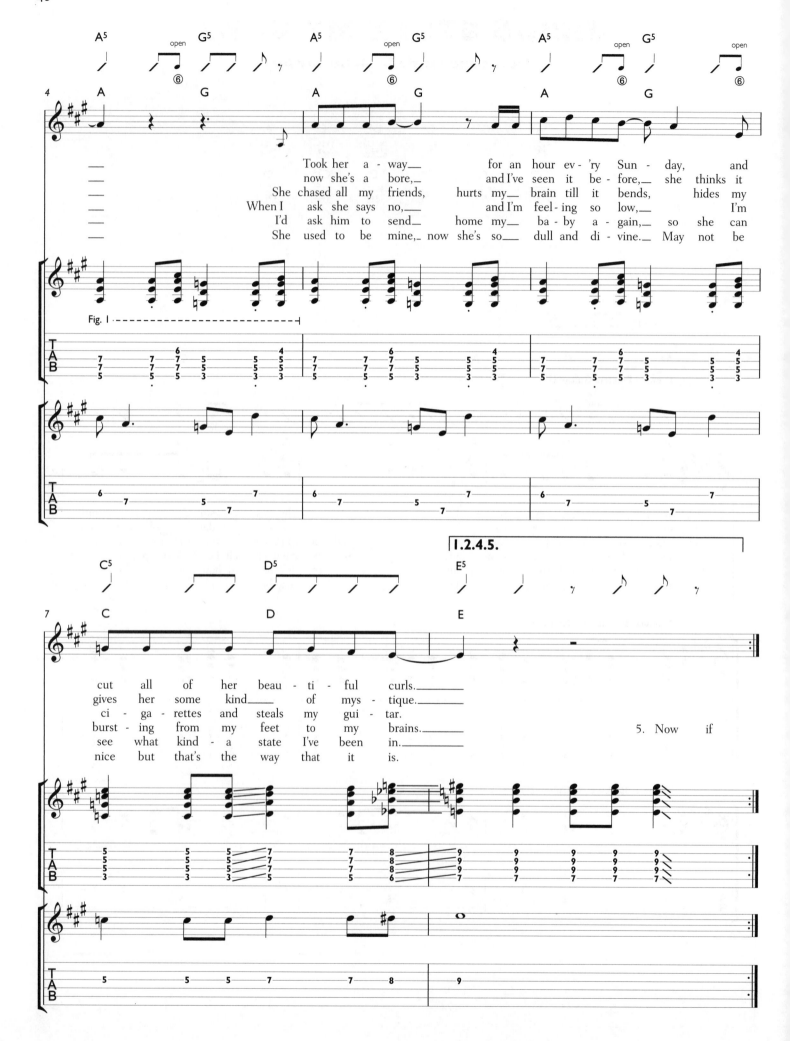

BABYDOLL

Words and Music by John Lawler

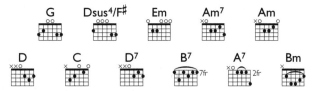

All music and chords with respect to capoed Gtr. 2rd fret
Song sounds in A

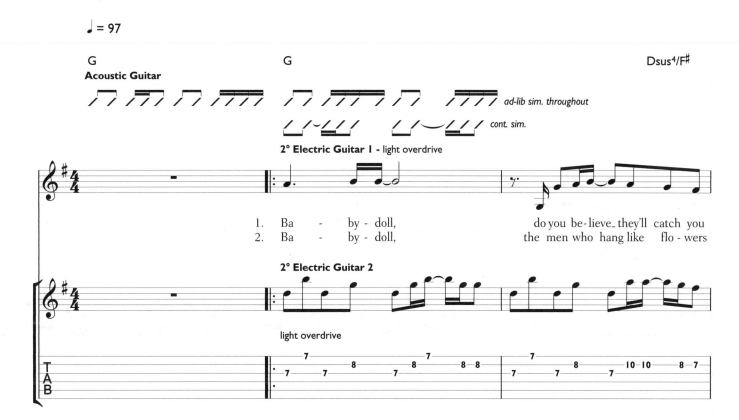

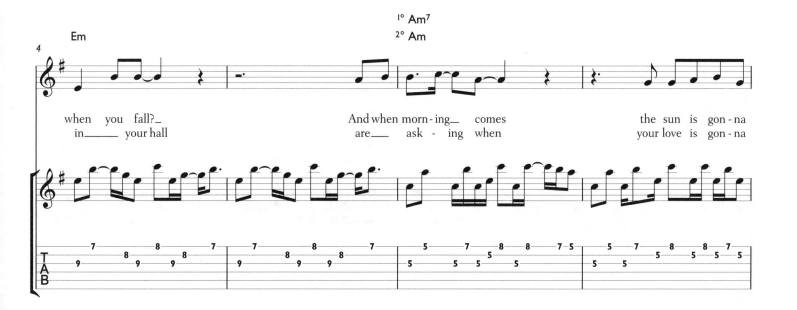

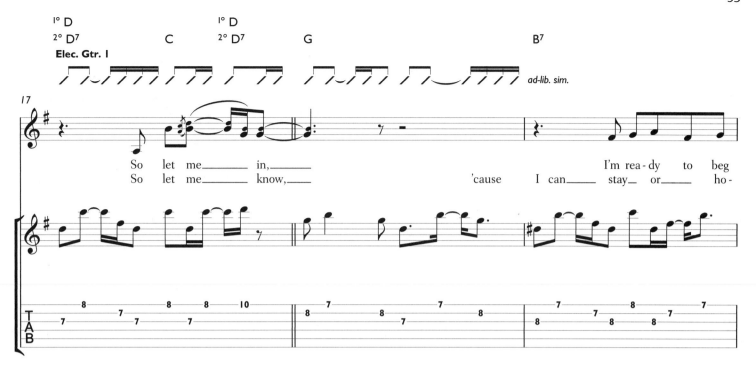

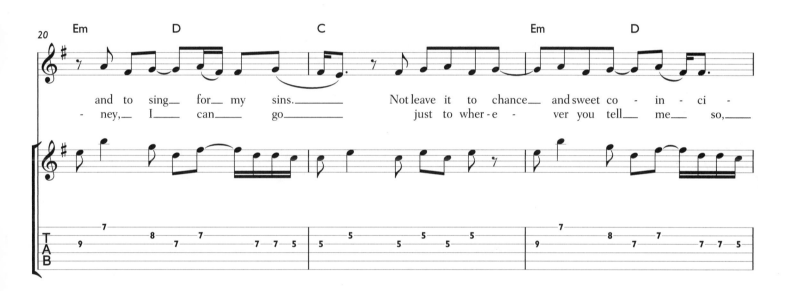

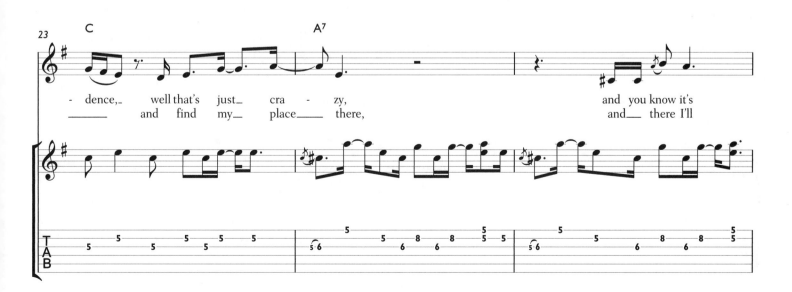

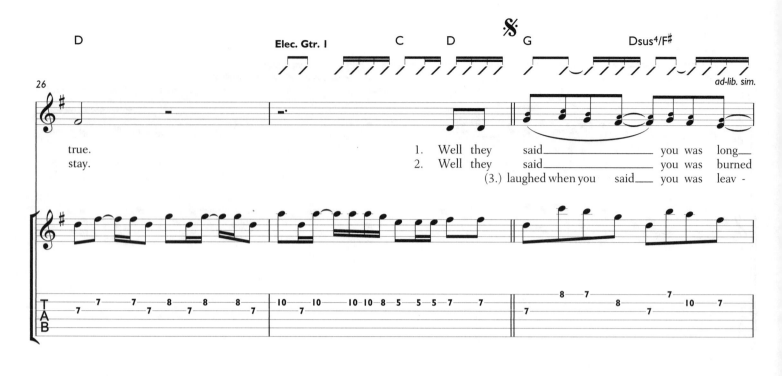

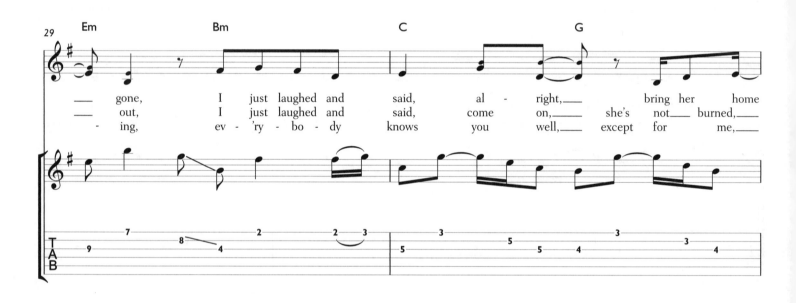

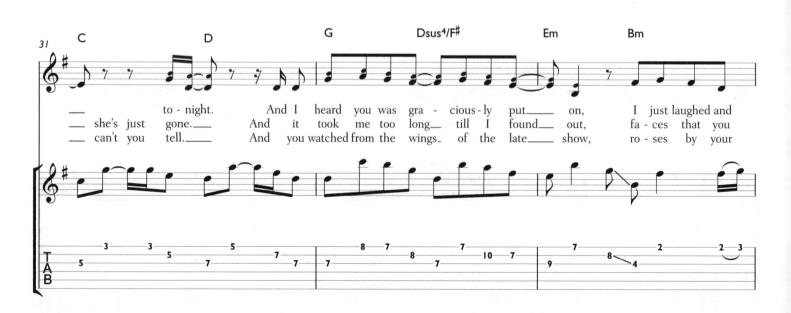

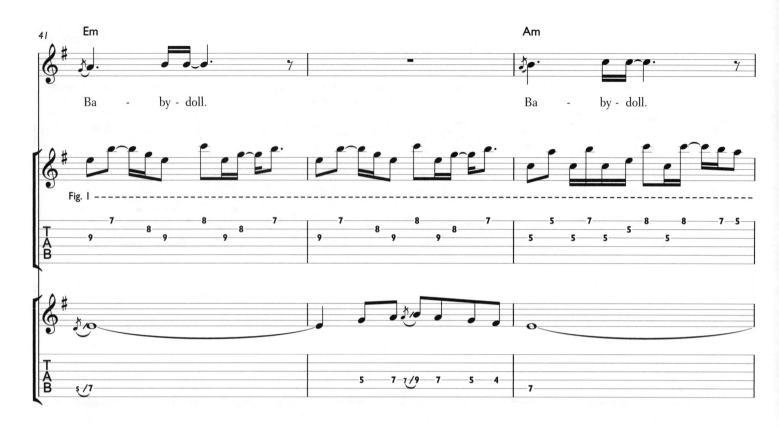

Ba - by - doll.   Ba - by - doll.

Ba - by - doll.

TELL ME A LIE

Words and Music by John Lawler

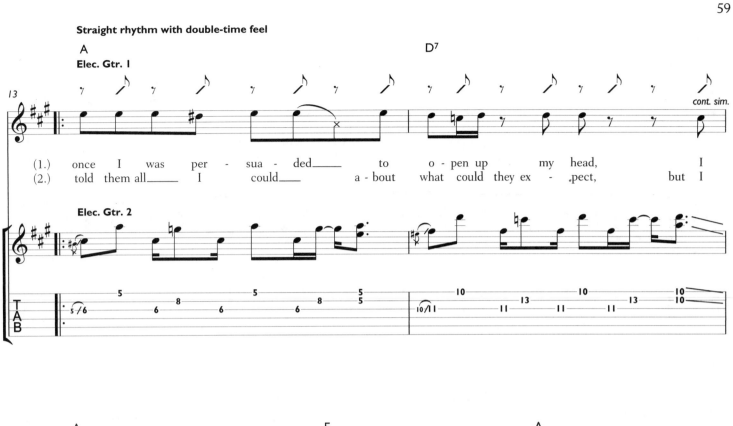

Straight rhythm with double-time feel

Elec. Gtr. 1

cont. sim.

(1.) once I was per - sua - ded_____ to o - pen up my head, I
(2.) told them all_____ I could_____ a - bout what could they ex - pect, but I

told them how it was and went and got it wrong__ in - stead. I said____would you be - lieve me
lost my sense of smell__ and I gained____ my self__ res - pect. They told____ me I was__ cu - ri - ous, I

if you on - ly knew I'd been steal - ing ev -'ry - thing, this con - ver - sa - tion's
told them they were slow. And they asked me where I get this stuff, I told them I__ don't

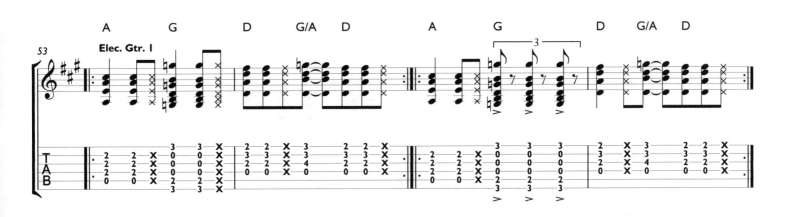

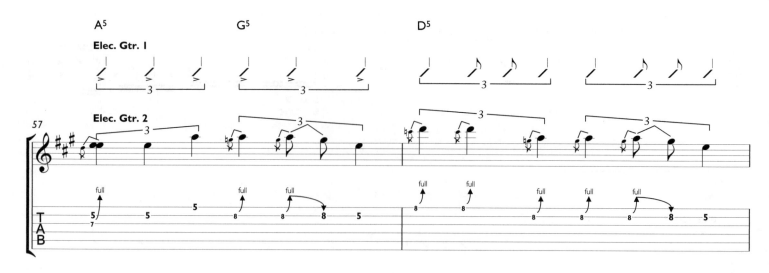

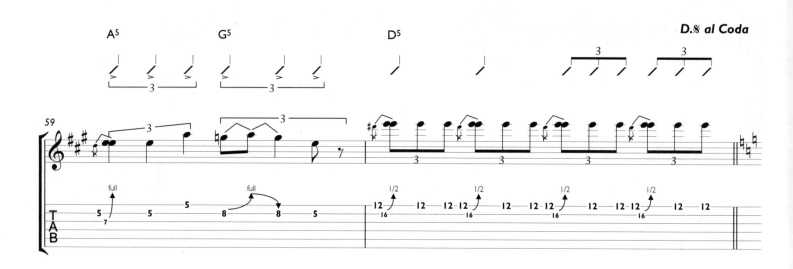

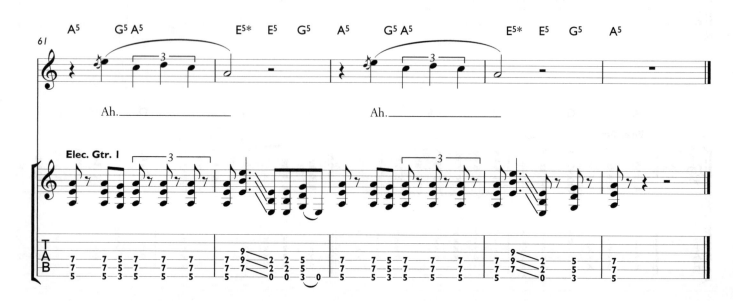

ACID JAZZ SINGER

Words and Music by John Lawler

Some said she was saint- ly, to some she was a swing- er, me I on- ly knew her as an a - cid jazz sing- er, come on.

To Coda

3. Well

let ring -----------------

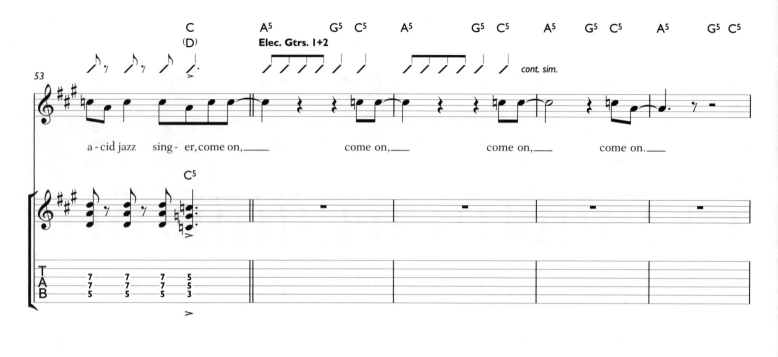

a-cid jazz sing-er, come on,____ come on,____ come on,____ come on.____

La la la la la la, oh la la la la, oh la la la la, oh la la la la, oh la la la la,

oh la la la la, la la la la la la, la la la la la la. Come on,____ come on,

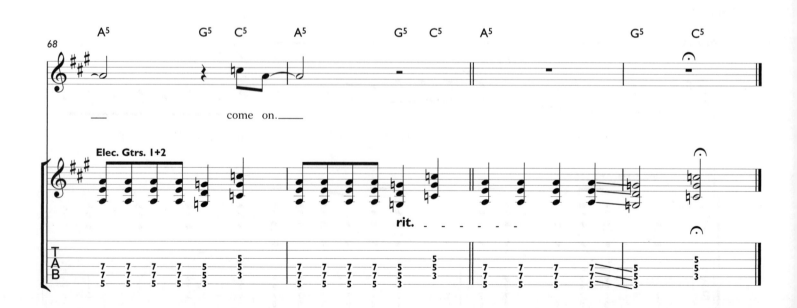

____ come on.____

LUPE BROWN

Words and Music by John Lawler

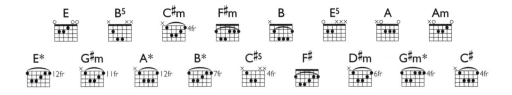

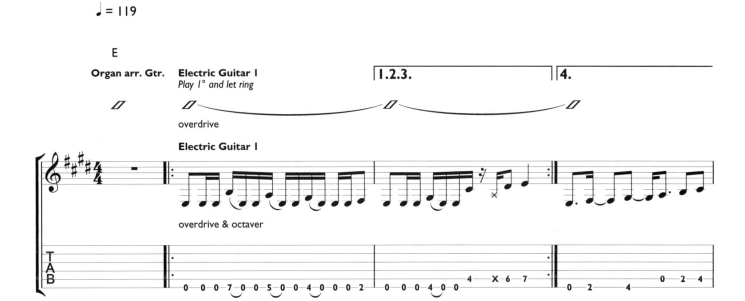

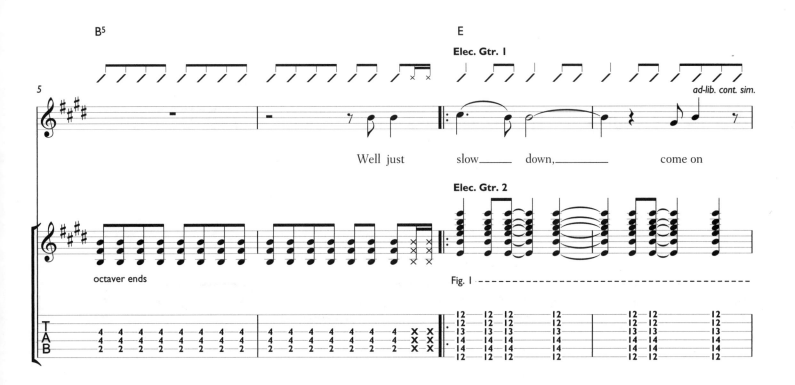

Lu - pe__ Brown,__ tell Des - de - mo - na that I'm rea - dy to leave, well she's

no - thing much to look at and she's hard to be - lieve. Well don't go_____ down,__

Elec. Gtr. 2 ad-lib. Fig. I

__ throw your arms a - round__ ev - 'ry lit - tle psy - cho that you

hap - pen to see, well you meant ev - 'ry - thing to them but you meant no - thing to me. { 1. Well your
{ 2. You got

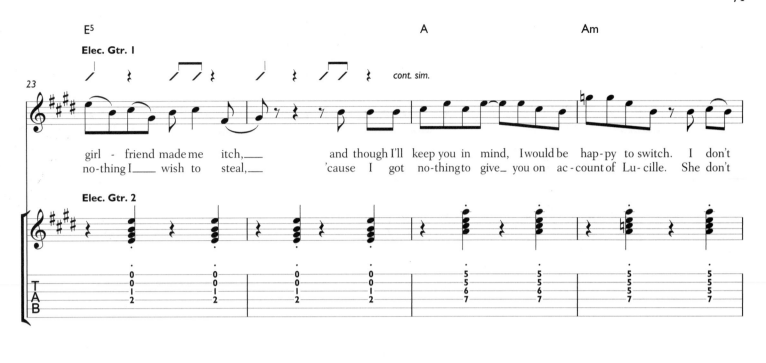

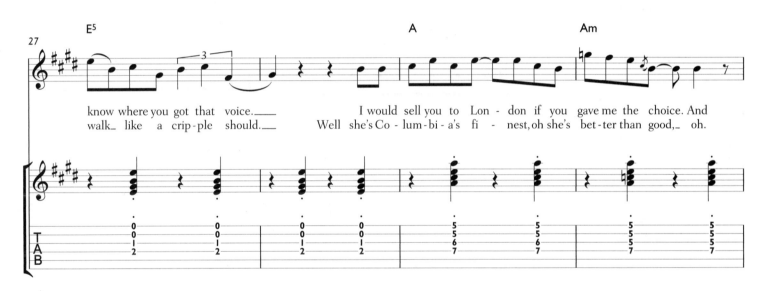

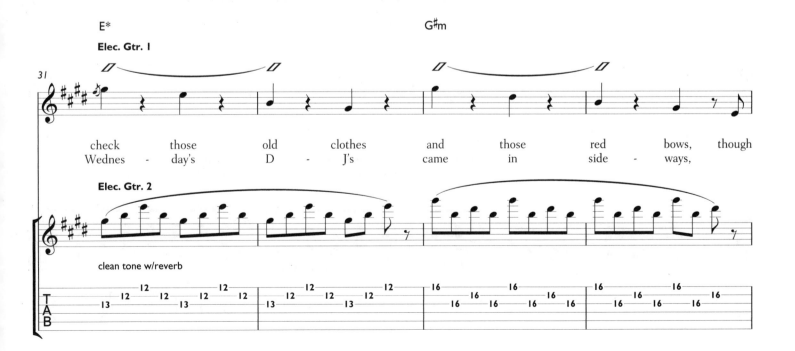

down,　Lu - pe—　Brown.—

— throw your arms a - round— ev - 'ry lit - tle psy-cho that you

hap - pen to see.　Well you meant ev - 'ry-thing to them but you meant no-thing to me.　(Well just)

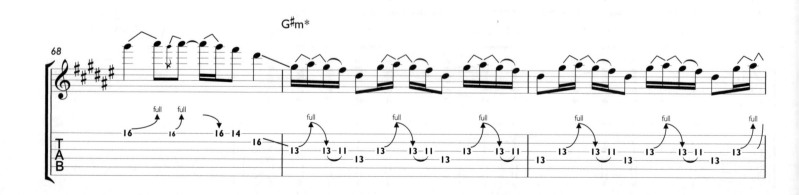

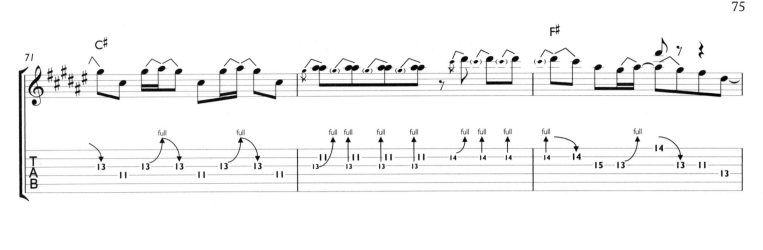

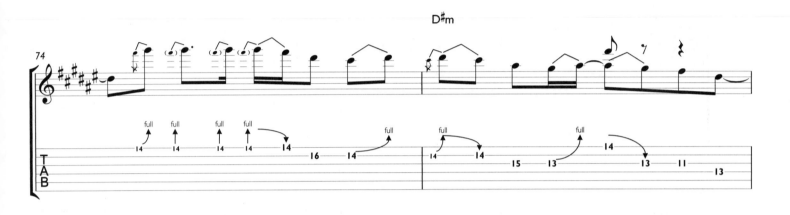

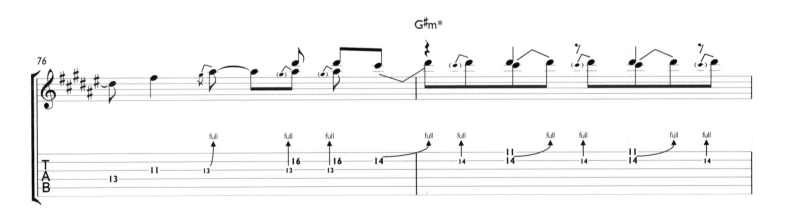

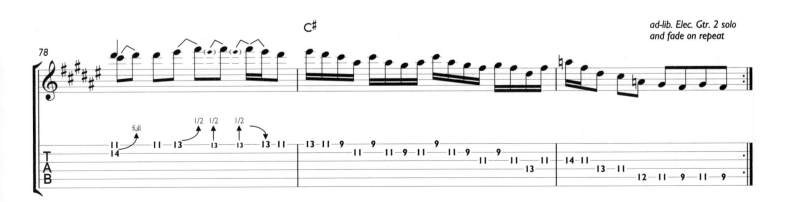

MILK AND MONEY

Words and Music by John Lawler

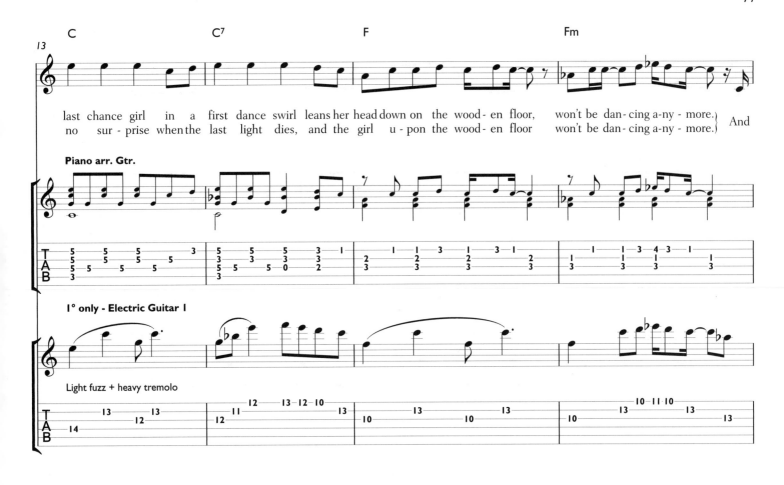

last chance girl   in   a   first dance swirl leans her head down on the wood - en floor,   won't be dan - cing a-ny - more. } And
no   sur - prise when the last   light   dies, and the girl   u - pon the wood - en floor   won't be dan - cing a-ny - more. }

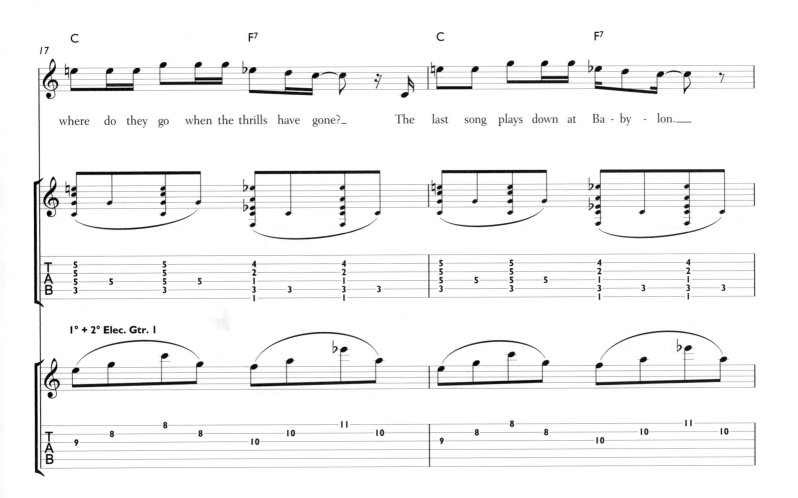

where   do   they   go   when the thrills have gone?_   The   last   song   plays   down   at   Ba - by - lon._

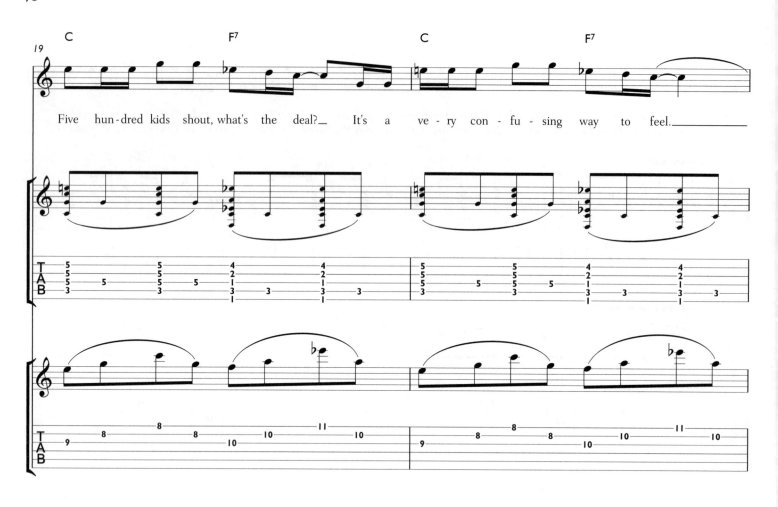

Five hun-dred kids shout, what's the deal?__ It's a ve - ry con - fu - sing way to feel._____

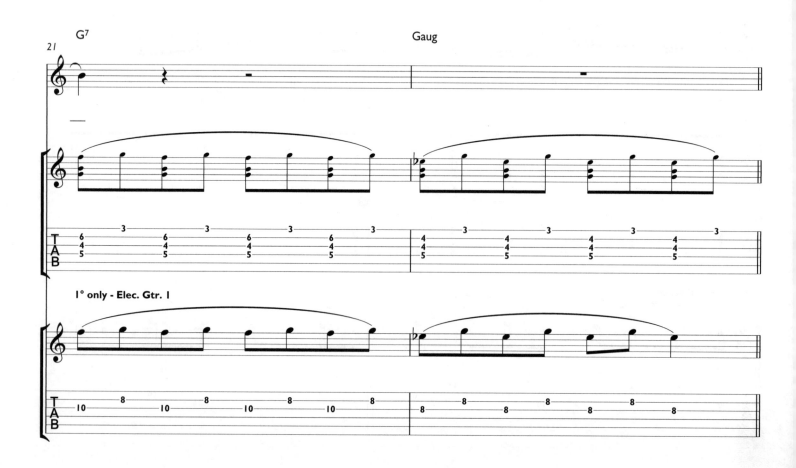

1° only - Elec. Gtr. 1

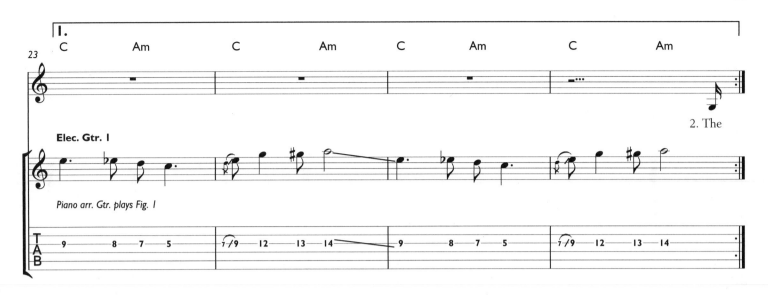

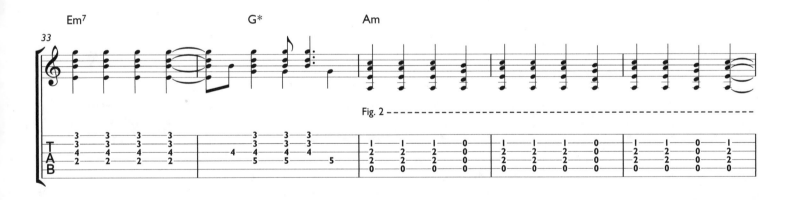

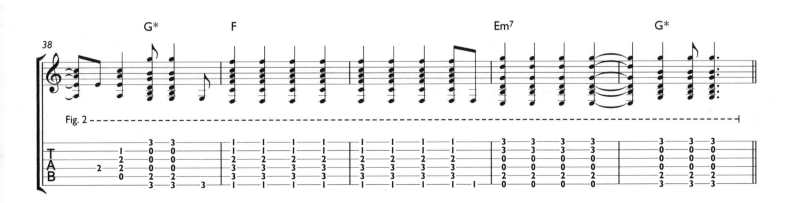

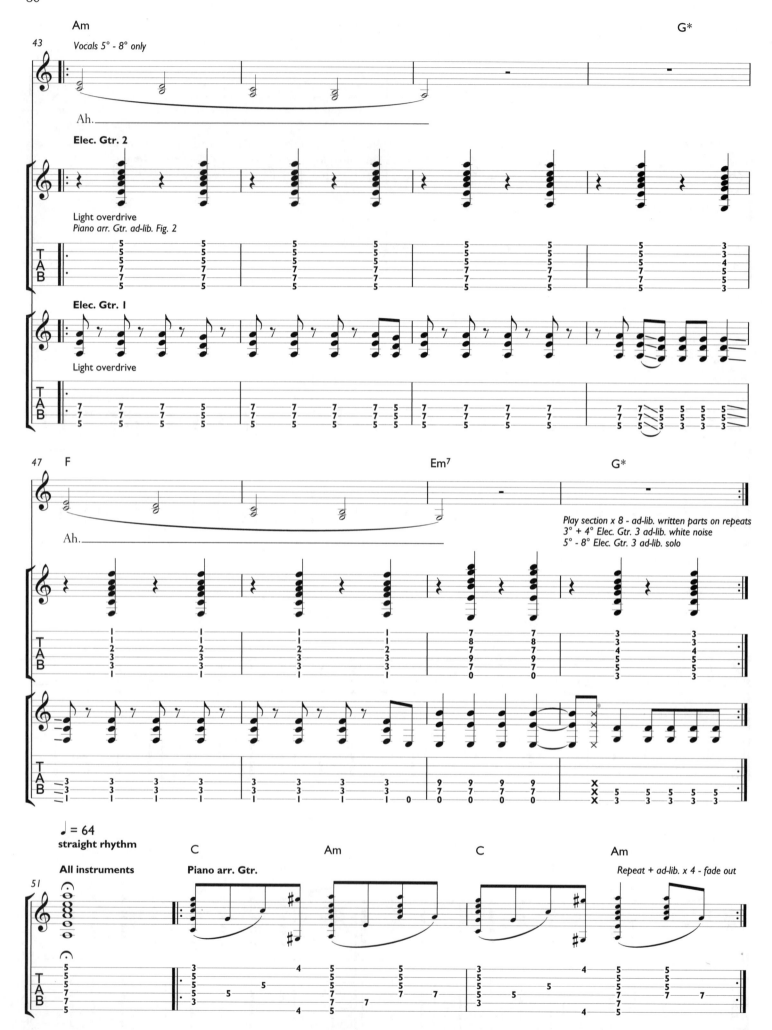

Notation and Tablature explained

Understanding chord boxes

Chord boxes show the neck of your guitar as if viewed head on—the vertical lines represent the strings (low E to high E, from left to right), and the horizontal lines represent the frets.

An **X** above a string means 'don't play this string'.
An **O** above a string means 'play this open string'.
The black dots show you where to put your fingers.

A curved line joining two dots on the fretboard represents a 'barre'. This means that you flatten one of your fingers (usually the first) so that you hold down all the strings between the two dots at the fret marked.

A fret marking at the side of the chord box shows you where chords that are played higher up the neck are located.

Tuning your guitar

The best way to tune your guitar is to use an electronic tuner. Alternatively, you can use relative tuning; this will ensure that your guitar is in tune with itself, but won't guarantee that you will be in tune with the original track (or any other musicians).

How to use relative tuning

Fret the low E string at the 5th fret and pluck; compare this with the sound of the open A string. The two notes should be in tune. If not, adjust the tuning of the A string until the two notes match.

Repeat this process for the other strings according to this diagram:

Note that the B string should match the note at the 4th fret of the G string, whereas all the other strings match the note at the 5th fret of the string below.

As a final check, ensure that the bottom E string and top E string are in tune with each other.

Detuning and Capo use

If the song uses an unconventional tuning, it will say so clearly at the top of the music, e.g. '6 = D' (tune string 6 to D) or 'detune guitar down by a semitone'. If a capo is used, it will tell you the fret number to which it must be attached. The standard notation will always be in the key at which the song sounds, but the guitar tab will take tuning changes into account. Just detune/add the capo and follow the fret numbers. The chord symbols will show the sounding chord above and the chord you actually play below in brackets.

Use of figures

In order to make the layout of scores clearer, figures that occur several times in a song will be numbered, e.g. 'Fig. 1', 'Fig. 2', etc. A dotted line underneath shows the extent of the 'figure'. When a phrase is to be played, it will be marked clearly in the score, along with the instrument that should play it.

Reading Guitar Tab

Guitar tablature illustrates the six strings of the guitar graphically, showing you where you put your fingers for each note or chord. It is always shown with a stave in standard musical notation above it. The guitar tablature stave has six lines, each of them representing a different string. The top line is the high E string, the second line being the B string, and so on. Instead of using note heads, guitar tab uses numbers which show the fret number to be stopped by the left hand. The rhythm is indicated underneath the tab stave. Ex. 1 (below) shows four examples of single notes.

Ex. 2 shows four different chords. The 3rd one (Asus4) should be played as a barre chord at the 5th fret. The 4th chord (C9) is a half, or jazz chord shape. You have to mute the string marked with an 'x' (the A string in this case) with a finger of your fretting hand in order to obtain the correct voicing.

Ex.1

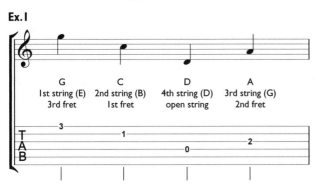

Ex.2

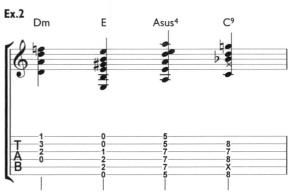

Notation of other guitar techniques

Picking hand techniques:

1. Down and up strokes
These symbols show that the first and third notes are to be played with a down stroke of the pick and the others up strokes.

2. Palm mute
Mute the notes with the palm of the picking hand by lightly touching the strings near the bridge.

3. Pick rake
Drag the pick across the indicated strings with a single sweep. The extra pressure will often mute the notes slightly and accentuate the final note.

4. Arpeggiated chords
Strum across the indicated strings in the direction of the arrow head of the wavy line.

5. Tremolo picking
Shown by the slashes on the stem of the note. Very fast alternate picking. Rapidly and continuously move the pick up and down on each note.

6. Pick scrape
Drag the edge of the pick up or down the lower strings to create a scraping sound.

7. Right hand tapping
'Tap' onto the note indicated by a '+' with a finger of the picking hand. It is nearly always followed by a pull-off to sound the note fretted below.

8. Tap slide
As with tapping, but the tapped note is slid randomly up the fretboard, then pulled off to the following note.

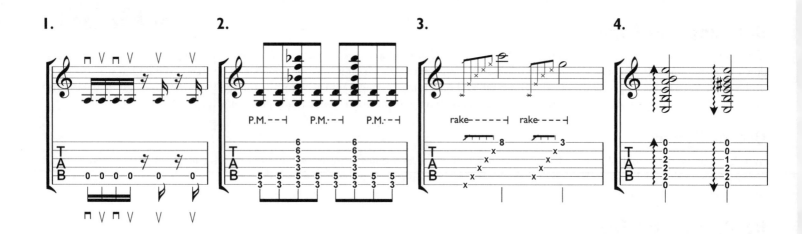

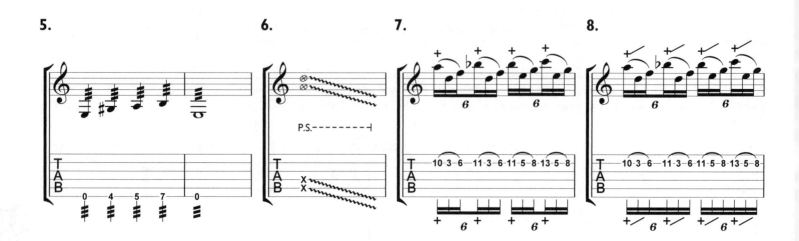

Fretting hand techniques:

I. Hammer-on and pull-off
These consist of two or more notes linked together by a slur. For hammer-ons, fret and play the lowest note, then 'hammer on' to the higher note with another finger. For a pull-off, play the highest note then 'pull off' to a lower note fretted with another finger. In both cases, only pick the first note.

2. Glissandi (slides)
Fret and pick the first note, then slide the finger up to the second note. If they are slurred together, do not re-pick the second note.

3. Slow glissando
Play the note(s) and slowly slide the finger(s) in the direction of the diagonal line(s).

4. Quick glissando
Play the note(s) and immediately slide the finger(s) in the direction of the diagonal line(s).

5. Trills
Play the note and rapidly alternate between this note and the nearest one above in the key signature. If a note in brackets is shown before, begin with this note.

6. Fret hand muting
Mute the notes with cross noteheads with the fretting hand.

7. Left hand tapping
Sound the note by tapping or hammering on to the note indicated by a 'o' with a finger of the fretting hand.

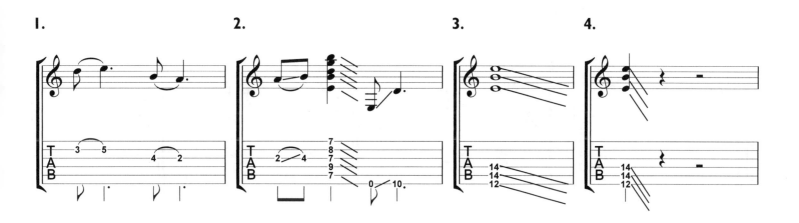

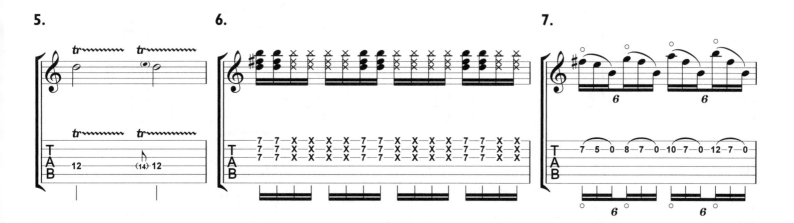

Bends and vibrato

Bends

Bends are shown by the curved arrow pointing to a number (in the tab).
Fret the first note and then bend the string up by the amount shown.

1. Semitone bend (half step bend)

The smallest conventional interval; equivalent to raising the note by one fret.

2. Whole tone bend (whole step bend)

Equivalent to two frets.

3. Minor third bend (whole step and a half)

Equivalent to three frets.

4. Microtonal bend (quarter-tone bend, Blues curl)

Bend by a slight degree, roughly equivalent to half a fret.

5. Bend and release

Fret and pick the first note. Bend up for the length of the note shown. May be followed by a release—letting the string fall back down to the original pitch.

6. Ghost bend (prebend)

Fret the bracketed note and bend quickly before picking the note.

7. Reverse bend

Fret the bracketed note and bend quickly before picking the note, immediately let fall back to the original.

8. Multiple bends

A series of bends and releases joined together. Only pick the first note.

9. Unison bend

Strike both indicated notes simultaneously and immediately bend the lower string up to the same pitch as the higher one.

10. Double note bend

Play both notes and bend simultaneously by the amount shown.

11. Bend involving more than one note

Bend first note and hold the bend whilst striking a note on another string.

12. Bends involving stationary notes

Play notes and bend lower string. Hold until release is indicated.

13. Vibrato

Shown by a wavy line. The fretting hand creates a vibrato effect using small, rapid up and down bends.

14. Bend and tap technique

Play and bend notes as shown, then sound final pitch by tapping onto note as indicated.

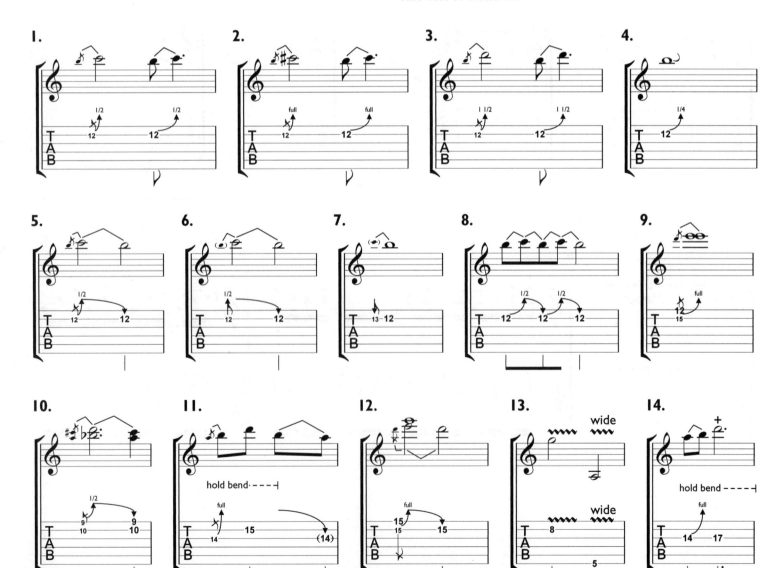